They Sha
The Spanisl
Mount's Bay, Cornwall
July 1595

Craig Weatherhill

First published in 2019 by:
Penwith Press
Cornwall
United Kingdom

www.penwithpress.co.uk

ISBN: 978-1-9997775-1-7

All rights reserved. For permission to reproduce any part of this book in any form or media, please contact the publisher.

Typesetting, design and layout:
Jonathan How
www.coherentvisions.com

PARS

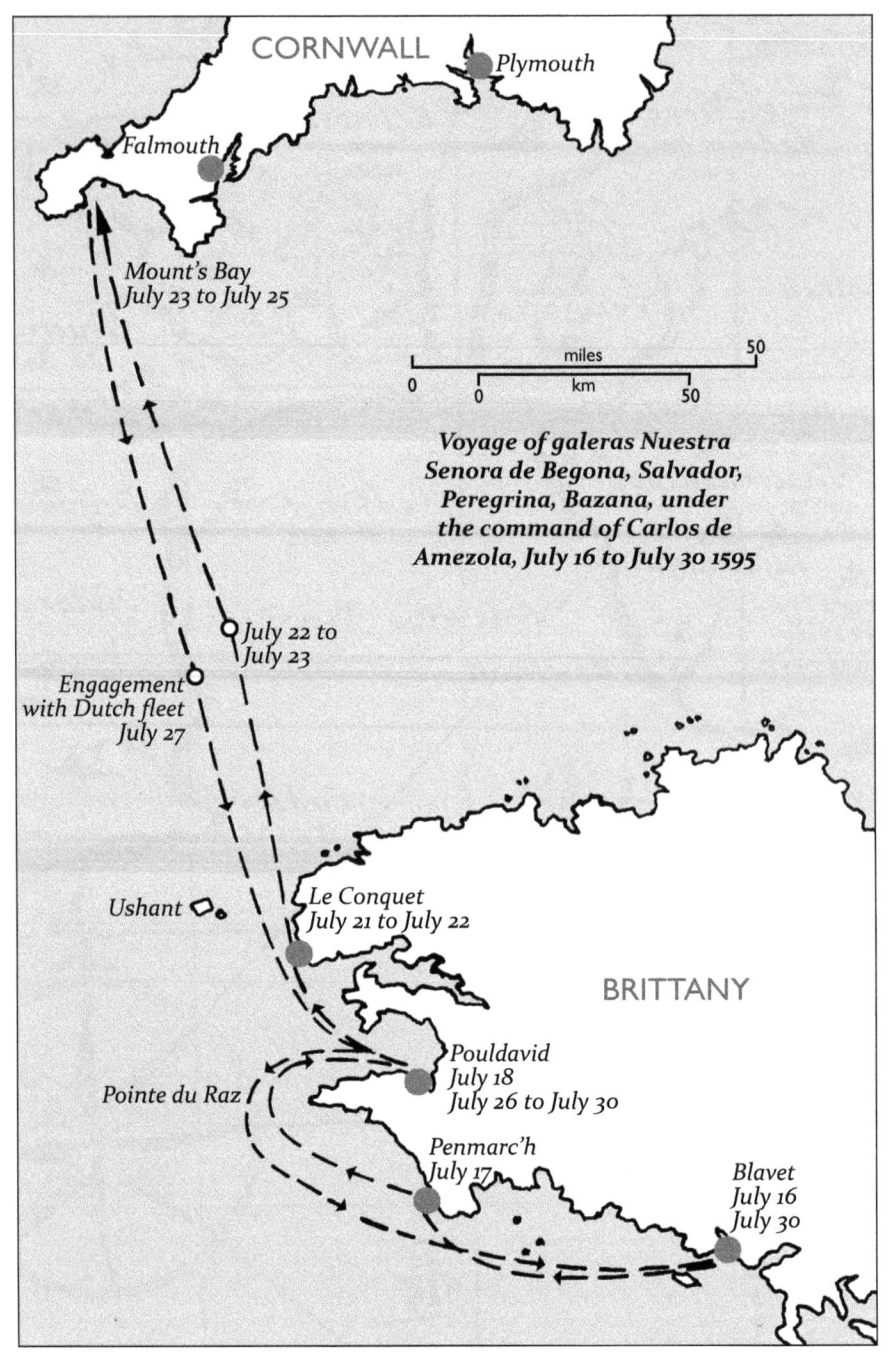

Contents

7	Foreword – Raglavar
9	Introduction
11	Reasons for the Raid
13	The Spanish Commander's Name
15	The Ships
17	The English Agent
18	The Port of Blavet
20	16th – 17th July 1595
21	18th July 1595
23	21st July 1595
24	22nd July 1595
25	22nd - 23rd July 1595: Overnight interlude
26	23rd July 1595: Morning
29	23rd July 1595: Afternoon
33	24th July 1595
35	25th July 1595
37	26th July 1595
39	30th July 1595
41	The Effects of the Raid
43	References

Foreword – Raglavar

This volume is sorely needed. The 'legend' of the 1595 Spanish Raid on Mount's Bay, Cornwall is much discussed within Cornish Studies and yet paradoxically no full history of events has previously been published. Craig Weatherhill's latest volume acts as a corrective to that oversight, and offers a definitive account of the Raid; not only discussing its origins, its context, its participants and its aftermath, but also locating it with the wider history of 'these islands'. The author – as with his previous works, such as the much acclaimed *Cornovia: Ancient Sites of Cornwall and Scilly* and *The Promontory People: An Early History of the Cornish* – offers a Cornu-centric response to this fascinating moment in the territory's complex history.

The Renaissance was clearly a time of great upheaval within Cornwall – both in terms of its engagement with external changes on the European continent – but also internally, with the linguistic and cultural shifts that the Age brought. These shifts and sways within the geo-political landscape of the territories on the Atlantic periphery of Europe offer us a context for the landings that took place in Mousehole, Paul, Newlyn and Penzance in the frantic summer of 1595.

Weatherhill has that unique ability as a writer and historian to locate this story within the wider history of the period, but as a distinguished expert on Cornish archaeology, topography and place-names he is also able to provide the reader with the precision of detail that would go unnoticed in other accounts. Although the main events of this volume took place well over four hundred years ago, their impact on the cultural geography and landscape of Cornwall are still noticeable. Certainly, the sea defences and castles of the peninsula that still remain show how problematical the threat from the Iberian Peninsula once was. Fortunately now, we live in more peaceful times.

I greatly commend this volume to you, the reader, as a significant contribution to the corpus of studies on Cornish history.

Alan M. Kent Ph.D., M.Phil, M.Ed., BA (Hons), PGCE, FHEA
Senior Lecturer in Literature, the Open University in South-West Britain
Visiting Fellow in Celtic Studies, University of A Coruña, Galicia, Spain

Newlyn and Penzance, 1540

Introduction

FOR a great many years, accounts of this singular event have been brief and incomplete. Mentions of it, such as those contained in F.E. Halliday's *A History of Cornwall* (1959) and P.A.S. Pool's *The History of the Town and Borough of Penzance* (1974) were based solely on the one-sided and, at best, second-hand account written by Richard Carew in his *A Survey of Cornwall* (1602), and on snippets of unconfirmed legend.

Carew was to write: *"Thus you have a summary report of the Spaniards' glorious enterprise and the Cornishmen's infamous cowardice"*, the seriously unfair opinion of a writer who was at no time within 70 miles of the event. Carew's rhetoric has needed to be tempered by fact recorded by an actual eye-witness to the whole affair. Who better than the Spanish commander himself?

That commander's subsequent report to King Philip II of Spain only came to light in the 1980s, and a translation by Robert Dickinson was published in the Journal of the Royal Institution of Cornwall in 1988. This report, when added to facts gleaned from Carew, Sir Nicholas Clifford, interrogations of the prisoners briefly held by the Spaniards, and other sources, can now give us a much fuller and more factual account of the raid.

Reasons for the Raid

THE Spanish authorities had several motives in mind when planning this daring venture. The drawn-out war between the thrones of Elizabeth I and Philip II had dealt them several blows, not least the disaster of the 1588 Armada. To land a force on the shores of Elizabeth I's realm, for at least as long a duration as Drake's 36-hour occupation of Cadiz in 1587, would be a major coup and a boost of morale to the Spanish nation and its navy.

The far west of Cornwall, 80 miles from the bulk of the British navy in Plymouth Sound, was a sound choice for a cross-channel incursion. Only 46 years earlier, a major Catholic insurrection against the State had erupted from Cornish soil, only to be put down after several bloody battles and appalling atrocities dealt out by overwhelming armed forces of the Crown, reinforced by mercenaries from Germany and Italy. Cornwall had also marched on London just over half a century earlier. Throughout Britain, Catholicism and resentment still simmered deep under the surface, and nowhere more so than in Cornwall.

An Italian agent in the employ of Philip II of Spain had written to the king, in a letter now in the Spanish State Papers held at the British Museum and pointed out this history. Like the Irish, he advised, the Cornish were not English and still strongly Catholic below the surface. A tempered invasion might provide the spark to either a further uprising, or an increase of collaboration with Spain.

Cornishman Tristram Wynslade, grandson of one of the leaders of the Cornish Catholic insurrection in 1549, also wrote to Philip II of Spain earlier in 1595, and enclosing a map, urging him to invade and restore Catholicism to Britain. He stated that many Cornish people would be supportive of such a move, although he made the mistake of naming Sir Francis Godolphin among that number!

A further incentive was a rumour that warehouses on Mount's Bay, in Mousehole or Penzance, might be housing the spoils of a Royal Navy raid on Pernambuco, Brazil. Warehouses in that port had held the valuable cargo of a Spanish East Indiaman that had struck an offshore reef. Under Admiral John Lancaster, a raiding party had gone ashore under cover of darkness to capture this cargo and ship it back to Britain. The Spanish authorities were determined to get it back.

A fourth aim of the mission was to conduct a detailed study of the Isles of Scilly, with a view to a Spanish capture of the islands for use as a naval base close to British shores. English prisoner Barnaby Loe of Ipswich, after his release from the galleys in Mount's Bay, told the home authorities that the galley flotilla had the intention of sailing, not only to Scilly, but to the Channel Islands, too, presumably a similar mission to assess them for suitability as a Spanish naval base. As it turned out, adverse winds prevented any voyage to the Channel Islands.

Newlyn, 1540

The Spanish Commander's Name

FOR some time, the name of this daring Spanish commander was unclear. Winston Graham, in *The Spanish Armadas* (1972), called him Don Carlos de Amésquita, this error being repeated by Pool, and others since then. The error appears to have been gleaned from a report written by Juan del Aguila y Arellano, Governor of Blavet (Port Louis, southern Brittany) from 1591 – 1598. This read as follows:

On 26th July (GB: 16th July) 1595, there sailed from Blavet 4 galleys of the squadron of Pedro de Zubiaur, which had in its charge the provisioning of the Biscay area. As part of their complement, three companies of arquebusiers boarded under the command of Captain Carlos de Amézqueta. After making port in Penmarc'h in order to stock up on provisions, they set sail at dawn on 31st July (GB: 21st July) and, on the 2nd August (GB: 23rd July), at dawn, they landed in Mount's Bay, between Capes Lizard and Cornwall. The infantry formed a squadron that advanced towards the neighbouring settlement of Mousehole, which was cannonaded in turn from the galleys. Mousehole, Newlyn, Saint Paul and the fort of Penzance were looted and burned in the days comprising the incursion. On 4th of August (GB: 25th July), after taking away the artillery piece from the fort, they moved away from the coast. On the following day, in the Channel, they came across a Dutch fleet of 46 sails but, before making peace, they even sank one or two enemy ships at the coast of 20 lives, the only losses of the expedition. Finally, they made repairs in Penmarc'h, then returned to Blavet. (Spanish dating then differed by 10 days from that used in Britain: the British dates are here entered in brackets).

Quite why Juan del Aguila miswrote the name of the commander remains a mystery but it is clear, from his own report, that the officer's name was, in fact, Carlos de Amézola. After all, the owner of the name is the ultimate authority. He refers to himself by that name throughout, and this correct version also appears in a letter written by King Philip II of Spain on 25th February 1596 (*"las galeras de Don Carlos de Amezola"*).

The surname is an interesting one. It appears to be a Spanish rendition of a Basque name: Ametzola . The settlement of Ametzola lies inland from the port and city of Bilbao, and has the apparent meaning of "plentiful in oaks". It is, therefore, a reasonable assumption that Captain Carlos de Amézola was himself a Basque, a race of people renowned for their seafaring skills. This appears to be confirmed by a list of notable Basques, which includes him under the sub-heading "Military".

English state papers from the reign of Elizabeth I habitually anglicise the Spanish names involved in the affair, listing Pedro de Zubiaur as "Peter Seviore", and Carlos de Amézola as "Charles de Messe".

The Ships

THE flotilla of four ships that took part in the raid consisted of war galleys (*galeras*). These were sleek vessels, powered by up to 70 oars in single banks, and large triangular lateen sails on (usually) two masts, rigged in much the same way as an Arabian dhow. Ordnance consisted of five guns mounted in the bow, so could only fire by turning bow-on to the target. The long, square-section bowsprit jutting from a beautifully graceful bow was set horizontally in order to avoid damage from this forward-directed fire.

These guns probably consisted of a central full cannon of 5,000-6,000 lbs weight, firing a 40-50lb ball, flanked on each side by a *sacre*, weighing 1,500-1,800 lbs each and firing balls of 7-13lbs weight. The starboard gun was usually a *pedrero*, 1,200-1,500 lbs in weight, and firing an 18-20lbs shot; and the port gun a half *sacre*, weighing about 1,000 lbs and loaded with a 4-5lbs ball. These were housed beneath a decked platform, or *arrumbada*, often equipped with four or five bronze swivel-mounted firearms.

The poop deck sloped upward to a high stern manned by the helmsman, who had charge of the tiller. In adverse weather, this poop deck was often roofed by canvas on hooped supports, and it was here where the captain and his senior officers were chiefly stationed. From the foot of the poop deck a central, open gangway, or *corsia*, ran forward to the foredeck between the rowing benches. The oar housing, or *apostis*, overhung the hull on both sides of the ship.

One of the prisoners released in Mount's Bay by Captain de Amézola was Barnaby Loe, a mariner from Ipswich, who had been taken from his own ship off the coast of Brittany some three weeks before the raid by Pedro de Zubiaur, and put to work – presumably at the oars – on de Amézola's flagship. He was able to describe the galleys as follows:

"*The shipping at Bluett* (Blavet) *consists of four galleys, whereof Charles de Messe* (Carlos de Amézola) *is general... Each of these galleys carries five pieces* (of ordnance) *in its prow, and 590 men and, for this voyage, had 400 soldiers out of Don John's* (Don Juan's) *regiment, besides 200 others. They can land 150 men at a time with their eight pinnaces and gondells, and can row 10 leagues a day against a good gale of wind.*"

The flagship of the flotilla, termed the *capitana*, was named *Nuestra Señora de Begoña*, (Our Lady of Begona), a further link with the Basque region. The 16th century Basílica de Nuestra Señora de Begoña is a major place of worship in the Basque city of Bilbao. The deputy flagship, or *patrona*, carried the name *Salvador*; the other galleys being named *Peregrina* and *Bazana*.

It is not known if the last-named was the same as the galley *Bazana* that had survived the disastrous Spanish Armada, seven years earlier, and returned home safely but, as the Spanish navy was unlikely to have had two galleys of the same name, it is probable. That galley was an estimated 95 feet (25m) in overall length, with a 25-foot (7.6m) beam. She had a crew of 72, plus 222 rowers (implying 74 oars, 37 to a side, with three men on each), and weighed around 190 tonnes unladen. It is likely that the other three galleys shared similar specifications.

Late 16th century Spanish galera *(galley)*

The English Agent

IN his 1602 account, Richard Carew failed to mention the presence, aboard the Spanish flagship, of Captain Richard Burley, referred to by Amézola as Ricardo Burley.

Carew's informants might have missed him but Barnaby Loe had not. On questioning after his release by the Spaniards, he told his English interrogators:

"They have an Englishman, Captain Burley of Weymouth, with them, whom they esteem; he sits next to the captain. He said that, if Her Majesty (Elizabeth I) *was not at extraordinary charge in keeping good forces, the King of Spain who, by his treasure, is so strong, would land such a power as should overcome the land; that those four galleys, with two others, would be yearly sent to spoil the weak places of this realm, and the isles adjoining, and that they might return again this summer."*

Burley, of whom little else is known, was evidently a committed Catholic; a faith outlawed in England on pain of death. That Burley was not alone in placing his loyalty in his faith, rather than his monarch, and pledging allegiance to Spain as a perceived champion of Roman Catholicism, was hinted at by one of Barnaby Loe's fellow prisoners aboard the galleys. This was Robert Kettell, sailor and barque-master from Liverpool. Kettell had been taken from his own vessel and forced to serve aboard the galley as pilot, particularly with a view to eventually guiding them into the Isles of Scilly.

"They have four or five pinnaces at Bluett (Blavet), *which they often send forth with Englishmen in them, to get intelligence to England and, by this means, have continual advice"*. This intelligence was evidently supplied to these agents by other disaffected Catholics on British shores.

Amézola himself mentions Burley in his report to Philip II, describing him as: "an English gentleman entertained in Your Majesty's Royal Navy". As an experienced mariner, intimately familiar with the southern coasts of Britain, Captain Burley was doubtless aboard the Spanish flagship to act as chief pilot and navigator.

The Port of Blavet

IN October 1590, just two years after the Armada, Philip II of Spain took advantage of the murder of Henry III of France in the previous year, by sending a force to occupy the port of Blavet (now Port Louis, across the estuary from the town of Lorient) on the southern coast of Brittany; his intention being to undermine the intentions of the Protestant (Huguenot) Henry de Navarre of accession to the throne of France.

Henry III had appointed his brother-in-law, the Duke of Mercoeur, to the post of Governor of Brittany. Mercoeur was one of many who proposed several Catholic pretenders to challenge Henry de Navarre's claim. In order to achieve this, he encouraged Philip II of Spain to claim that his daughter, Infanta Isabella Clara Eugenie, was the heir to the throne of France and the Duchy of Brittany, alleging that she was the grand-daughter of Henry II of France, himself the grandson of Ann, Duchess of Brittany.

The citizens of Blavet, however, rejected offers for them to join the ultra-Catholic Holy League opposing Henry de Navarre, preferring representation by the Lord of Coëtcourson, a strong supporter of Henry, who eventually made good his claim and was crowned Henry IV.

Mercoeur immediately besieged Blavet. He was initially pegged back by the defence line across the isthmus but, by sending troops in by sea, he took the town, slaughtering the inhabitants. He burned the town to the ground and then offered the port to his ally, Philip of Spain.

The garrison that he sent was considerable, consisting of 37 ships and close to 6,500 men. Four of the ships were sent back as being unsuitable for Biscay conditions, and were replaced by the four galleys that eventually raided Mount's Bay. The naval force at Blavet came under the overall command of Don Diego Brochero, while Don Juan del Aguila y Arellano was appointed as Governor, a position he held from 1590-98. It was the latter who commanded the rebuilding of old fortifications and the replacement of the former citadel with a new fort, to be called Fuerte del Aguila.

By 1595, all that remained stationed at Blavet were a number of flyboats, pinnaces and other light vessels that were used to maintain communications with Catholic agents in Britain and France and to attack passing convoys; and the four war galleys commanded by Don Carlos de Amézola.

It was Brochero was saw these four vessels as a means of inflicting damage upon British and Protestant interests, proposing that they become a unit that could launch damaging raids on British coasts and ports. The idea, and subsequent approval, for the Mount's Bay raid was born.

Le Fort de Blavet (Fuerte del Aquila), built 1590

16th – 17th July 1595

HAVING received their orders, the four galleys commanded by Carlos de Amézola set out from Blavet on the morning of 16th July 1595 (26th July in the Spanish reckoning of the time), with all the necessary troops aboard and enough provisions to last them for six weeks. They sailed on a north-westerly course for the full day in calm weather, finally anchoring in a spot two leagues off Penmarc'h (called Plezmarg by Amézola, and Penmarch by Juan del Aguila).

At dawn on the 17th July, the galleys weighed anchor and set sail for Penmarc'h, which Amézola knew to be under Protestant control. Arriving at 8am, the commander ordered the ships to heave-to, and instructed the Sergeant Major of the Galleys to man the launches and skiffs, and make a show of intending to attack the town.

As intended, this created alarm and three of the leading citizens hurried down to the quay to parley. Refreshment for Amézola's men was peacefully negotiated for an agreed fee, which was paid by paymaster Ambrosio Sambujero, who also held the post of Master of the Flagship.

The low-lying headland of Penmarc'h has a fascinating item of folklore that links it with Cornwall. It is here that the ghost of King Mark, the 6th century ruler of Cornwall and Brittany, is said to ride the wild Atlantic storms on a winged horse.

Keigwin Manor, Mousehole

18th July 1595

AFTER an overnight stay, the galleys continued their voyage, rounding the Pointe du Raz (entered in the commander's report as Cabo de Ras de Antenao) without incident. They were now heading for the port of Pouldavid (Pendavi in Amézola's report), now part of the port of Douarnenez, where they would encounter a thoroughly unpleasant individual.

Guy Éder de Beaumanoir de la Haye, known as La Fontenelle to his own men, and Ar Bleiz "the wolf" to the Breton people he had terrorized, was still just 22 years old.

Born into an old Breton family, he quickly learned the ways of the bullying privileged classes. He rose to command a band of young nobles and their followers, 400 strong, which ravaged the regions of Cornouaille and Trégor with indiscriminate looting, rape and wholesale mass murder. Eventually, with the wealth amassed from his looting, he occupied the fortress on the Île de Tristan at Douarnenez, forcing the local residents to demolish their own houses for material to strengthen his fortress. When thousands of local people reacted in anger, he is said to have killed 1,500 of them in just one day.

In the same year of the visit to Pouldavid of the four Spanish galleys, he abducted Marie le Chevoir of Coadélan, the heiress of a marquis. He first raped, and then married her. The girl was just 8 years old but remained with him until his death 7 years later.

Guy eventually came to the sticky end he so richly deserved. Although pardoned for all his crimes by Henry IV in 1598, he was later accused of conspiracy and sentenced to end his rapacious life shrieking on the horrific breaking wheel in the Place de Grève in Paris in September 1602.

This, then, was the youthful monster that Captain Carlos de Amézola was to meet at Pouldavid. He was, however, friendly towards the Spanish garrison at Blavet, and had arranged with Blavet's governor to provide the galleys with a quantity of biscuit. Nonetheless, Juan del Aguila also had the measure of the man and, in the pre-voyage briefing, had instructed Amézola to negotiate with care. He correctly anticipated that la Fontenelle would demand gunpowder as payment and instructed his commander to give as little as possible. Del Aguila needed to keep the man sweet: he was, after all, in control of a major port in a strategic position between Blavet and the rich pickings of Dutch and British cargo convoys plying the Channel.

As it turned out, la Fontenelle initially demanded 20 quintals (roughly 920 kg or 2028lbs), but Amézola showed true Basque resolve in the bargaining. Arguing that the needs of his galleys came first, he knocked down the demand until la Fontenelle reluctantly accepted an offer of 4 quintals (184kg or 405lbs) of gunpowder.

Mousehole and Paul, 1540

21st July 1595

ONE can imagine that Captain Carlos de Amézola sailed from Pouldavid and out of the bay of Douarnenez with a sour taste in his mouth after the previous day's haggling with a man like Guy Éder de la Fontenelle. At least, he now had his back to the man, and fresh sea air in his lungs as the galleys continued north-westward, and there would soon be an opportunity to amuse himself and his men.

Passing the entrance to Brest harbour, Amézola took his flotilla through the channel between the port of le Conquet and the offshore islands, and close enough to the port to provoke a degree of panic in the town. He was to write that the townspeople armed themselves and crowded down to the shore, making a great uproar and a show of defence. The Captain had no intention of attacking and sailed his fleet past the port, probably prudently keeping his galleys just out of range, but close enough to create the alarm that he had intended.

By now, a head wind had strengthened, and Amézola ordered his ships, under oar, to make for shelter under a headland 5 or 6 miles north of le Conquet. The townspeople of le Conquet followed them north along the coast, stirring up the countryfolk who congregated on the low clifftops, waving flags and brandishing arms. Again, the captain would have ensured that his ships remained out of range, always assuming that any of the firearms being threateningly brandished by members of the crowd actually worked. Once again, he saw no reason to inflict unnecessary harm, and ensured that none of the four galleys fired a single shot.

The ships remained there until 5pm, when the wind weakened and the sea became calm enough to them to continue their voyage, again under oar, through the night and until dawn.

By now, it was clear that the Spanish strategists who had planned the raid had also devised a plan to deflect attention from Mount's Bay by sending other ships to Falmouth Bay.

At 9pm, Thomas Luke and William Paskowe sent a message from Falmouth to Sir Francis Godolphin, Lord-Lieutenant of Cornwall, that 60 Spanish vessels were in the bay, off the reef known as The Manacles, and had been there all day. Two pinnaces had briefly approached the mouth of Falmouth harbour, but had then turned back to the fleet. They assured Sir Francis that a close watch would be kept, and that they would try to determine the purpose of the fleet's appearance.

22nd July 1595

AS dawn broke, Captain de Amézola's galleys sighted a small vessel from le Conquet, and the flagship, the *Nuestra Señora de Begoña*, broke away from the flotilla in pursuit. Within an hour, the vessel had been overtaken and captured. The crew and her cargo of wine were taken aboard the flagship, and Amézola set about interrogating the prisoners.

From them he learned that an English ship had visited le Conquet, in search of the Spanish naval base on the southern coast of Brittany and, on discovering that Amézola's four galleys had been to Penmarc'h, had left again in a hurry. He also learned that ships of the Royal Navy were in Falmouth, Dartmouth and Plymouth.

Putting the prisoners to work on the galleys, Amézola then ordered the captured vessel to be scuttled, whereupon she went to the bottom.

Meanwhile, in Falmouth, the Spanish diversionary tactics continued to be effective. Thomas Luke sent a second message to Sir Francis Godolphin, informing him that up to 20 enemy ships had been about the harbour the previous evening. He was now sending a boat out to take a closer look at them, promising to inform him further when she returned.

The galleys had now commenced their crossing to Britain, rowing until 10am, at which time a fresh west-south-west wind gave them the opportunity to ship oars and raise the great lateen sails. This allowed them steady progress until 9pm, at which point the pilots advised that, as they had not yet sighted land, it would be best to slow up and avoid making landfall at night.

The captain ordered the galleys to heave-to, but this was to be an anxious time. The wind had strengthened and the seas were rising to the point where conditions were becoming hazardous, the streamlined galleys having a low freeboard which risked them being swamped in a heavy sea. Nonetheless, they weathered the conditions without mishap until a signal by lantern from the stern of the flagship ordered a resumption of the voyage under sail.

22nd - 23rd July 1595: Overnight interlude

WAR between Britain and Spain had now been waged for ten years, and would not end for another nine but, as far as Cornwall was concerned, it had largely passed them by. None of the Spanish Armada's engagements with the Royal Navy, seven years earlier, had taken place off Cornwall and, contrary to popular myth, no Armada vessel foundered on Cornish shores.

Isolated incidents had taken place. Only two months earlier, a Spanish ship had captured the crew of a fishing boat from St Keverne parish, and only a week or two had gone by since a threatened landing of Spanish forces near Padstow had been successfully deterred by a waiting force of men led by one of the Grenville family from Stowe.

A legend exists of a supposed Spanish landing near Sennen Cove that caused the miller of Vellandreath and his son to flee away up the steep, sandy hill, carrying full sacks of flour on their backs for protection; sacks they were eventually forced to drop due to the additional weight of lead shot that had hit them without harming either man. This episode escapes us as recorded historical fact, but it would seem entirely plausible.

To the people of western Mount's Bay, these recorded incidents, the ships currently menacing Falmouth Bay, and even the war itself, would have seemed half a world away. What was about to hit them would come as an almighty shock.

23rd July 1595: Morning

EARLY in the morning, the galleys sighted land, evidently in clear conditions. Richard Carew, 80 miles from the spot, was the only person to assert that sunrise drove away a mist that screened the approach of the galleys which, in fact, had been seen by local people on the cliffs (probably from what is still named as Point Spaniard); a fact which was noted by Captain Carlos de Amézola who, as he wrote his report, could clearly see the coasts to the south of Mousehole, and the Lizard, away to starboard. Navigation had been precise enough to ensure that the galleys made a perfect entrance to Mount's Bay, close to its western coast.

Military precision and measured haste needed to be the order of the day. Spanish intelligence had been efficient, and de Amézola knew that the local militia was commanded by Sir Francis Godolphin. He further knew that Godolphin was also in charge of the forts on the Isles of Scilly, which were also on the mission's agenda.

The galleys hove-to off Mousehole at 8am, and immediately began to put their infantrymen ashore. First to set foot on enemy soil were Captain Don Léon Dezpeleta and his sergeant major Juan de Arnica, who lined up his men – 400 arquebusiers and some pikemen – to advance in two flanking movements to either side of the village. The left flank was to be led by Martin Ramirez de Arellano, subaltern of Don Luis de Maeda; the right by Juan de Urbea, subaltern of Don Gaspar de Perea.

This manoeuvre, up the steep hillsides to either side of the village, which Captain de Amézola estimated as containing at least 200 houses, not only allowed the landing forces to gain enough for them to gain a good view of the surrounding countryside, but left the village clear for the galleys to open fire on. Turning their bows towards shore, all four vessels opened fire on the village, the shot slamming into the houses and forcing the terrified inhabitants to flee.

A cessation of fire then allowed the landing force, probably that which had flanked the south side of the village to move in and put the settlement to the torch. It was at this point that the first Cornishman was to die.

This was Jenkin Keigwin, Mousehole's leading citizen, whose substantial stone house would be the only building to survive, as it does to the present day. Most other houses in the village would have been constructed of cob, timber and thatch, and would have burned far more easily. It is often alleged that Keigwin was killed by a cannonball which was afterwards kept preserved in the house, but it is more likely that his seniority allowed him to be one of a very few to own a firearm. If he had emerged from the house with a loaded firearm to offer a defence, then it was likely that he would immediately be shot by a Spanish arquebusier.

It would appear that Carlos de Amézola intended to keep Cornish casualties to an absolute minimum, perhaps to ensure a sympathetic response from local Catholics if another uprising against the Protestant Tudor state was to be forthcoming. The vast majority of local residents were unlikely to arm themselves with anything more than pitchforks and billhooks, hardly a threat to well-trained, professional soldiers. They could offer little more than a show of defence and would be allowed to escape with their lives.

The right flank of the landing force continued uphill to the village of Paul, which they set ablaze. The main target here was the parish church, contemptuously described by Amézola as a *mesquita*, "mosque", the Catholic Spaniards evidently viewing Protestantism with the same distaste they held for Islamic places of worship, after Spain's long occupation by the Islamic Moors of North Africa.

Many local people had gathered in the church for shelter, but were forced to flee again as the Spanish militia poured in. On receiving reports from the landing parties, Amézola was to describe a curious feature that his men had seen at the church in Paul:

"...in which there was a horse carved in wood and greatly embellished, serving as an idol worshipped by the people."

This begs the question: was this an 'Obby 'Oss of the kind which still parades through the streets of Padstow on May Day? Or was it another type of ceremonial horse effigy, such as the Penglaze ("grey head"), a sinister figure similar to the Mari Llwyd of Wales, which was brought onto the streets of Penzance at Christmas, and which has been revived in recent years? Whatever the answer, it was a curious thing to find within the puritan austerity of a Protestant church that despised idolatry.

The tower, south porch and some pillars of the nave of Paul church survived the assault, and a blackened arch can still be seen behind the present pulpit. The parish registers perished in the blaze, forcing the vicar, John Tremearne, to begin new registers, which he commenced on the following day.

Legends persist of a local woman finding a Spanish soldier asleep under a hedge and slitting his throat, and that Jenkin Keigwin killed members of the Spanish landing party before being fatally shot, but Amézola's report is clear that his force suffered no casualties at all until the journey home to Blavet.

Another story tells that a local farmer saved his own farm by setting light to his own furze-rick, fooling the Spaniards into believing that their own number had set fire to the farm itself.

While the sacking of Mousehole and Paul were under way, Captain de Amézola had ordered Captain Juan de Mercado to pull his galley, the *Peregrina*, clear of Penlee Point to check that no naval ships were lying off Newlyn or Penzance. He kept his vessel there for two hours until the flagship recalled him by the firing of a gun. A similar signal then recalled the shore parties who re-embarked.

In the meantime, Sir Francis Godolphin had become aware that something was gravely wrong. He had left his house, Godolphin House near Germoe, some 6 miles to the east of Penzance, that morning to settle a local dispute. From the hills, he could see gouts of smoke rising from the burning villages of Mousehole and Paul and, perhaps even the galleys themselves. Gathering as many men as he could at short notice, Godolphin hurried towards Penzance.

A smoke-blackened pillar in Paul church

23rd July 1595: Afternoon

THE galleys moved away from Mousehole, setting their course for Penzance and landing parties on the sand-dunes of the Western Green, which separated the town from Newlyn.

According to Carew's account, gleaned from Sir Francis Godolphin, the Spanish forces, some 400 strong, took up position on a hillslope, probably just west of the Lariggan stream, with two ranks of three soldiers being sent to the top to spy out the land. There is a large discrepancy between Carew's and Amézola's accounts regarding the number of defenders under Godolphin's command. Carew stated that it was something above a hundred, with 30 or 40 of them bearing firearms, adding that scarcely a third of those weapons were actually serviceable. Godolphin himself stated he had assembled about 200 men and was hoping for more to arrive. Amézola's report bafflingly gives the number as 1,200. If it can be assumed that this was a mistake, by a man who had remained on his vessel, for 200, then this would tally with Godolphin who was, at least, on the ground, and explain subsequent events much more easily, as even this number of ill-equipped men were outnumbered two-to-one by the heavily armed and well trained Spaniards.

At 1pm, from the town end of the Western Green, Sir Francis Godolphin and Thomas Chiverton of Kerris dispatched an urgent message to Sir Francis Drake and Sir John Hawkins at Plymouth:

"Four galleys are at anchor before Mousehole, their men landed, and the town and other houses in the country are fired. No more of the fleet are in sight. 50 or 60 were seen Monday evening and yesterday, athwart of Falmouth. Pray consider what is to be done both for safety and defence. PS: About 200 men are assembled; we attend the coming of more, so as to make head towards the enemy."

Restricted to only the most basic of weapons, a small number of firearms (most of which were useless and only carried in a show of bluff), and just a handful of horsemen, it was a pitiful defence force. Rather than condemn their eventual capitulation, as absent commentators were to do, the bravery of the local men's advance upon the Spanish forces should be admired. It was to be a short-lived show of defence. Godolphin had initially ordered his men to withdraw into the town from the exposed area of the Western Green, and to defend Penzance from within until reinforcements could arrive. However, the townsfolk had seen Mousehole and Paul go up in flames and were not prepared to see their own houses go the same way. They insisted upon marching across the Western Green to meet the Spaniards head-on – an incredibly brave but, ultimately, foolhardy decision.

The Spanish forces again took to dividing into flanks, forming a pincer movement. The galleys, which had been anchored closer to Newlyn than Penzance, moved in menacingly, turning bow-on to shore to bombard the defenders with shot. On shore, Captain Don Léon ordered his subaltern Juan de Urbea to move forward with the right, seaward, flank to force the defenders back, giving him the help of some musketeers.

It was all too much for the local men, who turned and ran for the shelter of the town. Several flung themselves down as the Spanish fire from both soldiers and galleys rained in around them. It seemed, however, that the Spaniards were intent upon causing as little harm as possible, firing to cause alarm and panic, and not to kill. Godolphin, via Carew, stated that none of his men had been hurt, except a constable who was flung from his horse without injury when a musket ball creased his doublet.

Amézola wrote in his report that his forces suffered neither loss nor injury, but that 50 of the town's defenders had been killed, which conflicts with Godolphin's account. It may be that, from his offshore position on the flagship, he had seen men flinging themselves down to avoid the gunfire and wrongly assumed they had succumbed.

Sir Francis Godolphin proposed making a stand against the advancing Spaniards in the town's market place but, by then, the townspeople had seen more than enough. Sir Francis found himself accompanied by just two musketeers and a dozen others, many of them his own servants. Persuasion, and even threats with a drawn rapier, against the remainder proved useless, and he was left with no choice but to realise that his position was hopeless. His only option was to leave the town to its doom, withdraw to Marazion Green to prepare for the defence of that town and St Michael's Mount, and await reinforcements. Behind him, the Spanish soldiers entered Penzance at three points, and began to put it to the torch.

Amézola noted that many of the houses in Penzance were well built and seemingly in wealthy ownership but, nonetheless, more than 400 of them were razed to the ground. His men also set fire to a shore battery containing a single gun, and to three ships in the harbour which were laden with wine and other cargoes, while some outlying farms and hamlets met with the same fiery fate. One of the burnt ships had aboard three newly recast bells for Paul church, the tower of which had survived the morning's blaze.

The church of St Mary's, above the harbour, was spared at the plea of Captain Richard Burley, the Weymouth Catholic who served in King Philip II's navy, and who had been at Captain de Amézola's side throughout the voyage. He insisted that the church had been Catholic, with Mass being held there, perhaps a memory from a previous visit as a shipmaster. The chaplain of the galleys, Friar Domingo Martinez, then wrote two paragraphs in English on a scrap of parchment, explaining why the church had been spared and expressing his trust in God that Mass would be celebrated there again, within two years, and under Spanish rule. This was nailed to the door.

By now it was late in the afternoon. The Spanish forces now turned their attention to Newlyn which, like Mousehole, Paul and Penzance before it, ended the day in ashes. It had been a devastating raid, planned and executed with a precision that can only be marvelled at. Four settlements lay in ruin, and Captain Carlos de Amézola had not lost a single man under his overall command.

As night set in, the Captain thought it prudent to take his galleys out of Mount's Bay, amusing himself by sailing aimlessly through the night, under a south westerly wind, to look for shipping.

By evening, Hannibal Vyvyan, commanding St Mawes Castle, had received a report of the day's events, and immediately sent a dispatch to Sir Francis Drake and Sir John Hawkins, commanding the Royal Navy fleet in Plymouth, and making rather an unfair judgement:

"I think you are informed of the Spaniards landing this day in the western parts: they have burned Penzance, Newlyn, Paul church and churchtown, and other villages adjoining without resistance; I speak it to the disgrace of those people. The only ships there are four galleys, but there are 40 sail seen to seaward. There is great want of leaders; the Spaniards' conquest without resistance may give them greater encouragement to land along the coast as well to the east as north. I beg you, if your ships are not fit to fight, to send into these parts some of their leaders who have commanded in war, as they are greatly needed now, and will be more so if the Spaniards should land. If you lack mariners, I think 100 could be procured in 10 hours in Falmouth harbour."

Carew was equally unfair, writing of the Cornishmen's *"infamous cowardice, which (were there any cause) I could qualify by many reasons: as, the suddenness of the attempt, the narrowness of the country, the openness of the town, the advantage of the galleys' ordnance on a people unprepared against such accidents through our long continued peace and at that very time for the most part either in their tin-works or at sea, who ere the next day made a resistance even with a handful, and entered a vowed resolution to revenge their loss at the next encounter if the enemy had landed again".* However, Carew then backtracks, admitting that: *"all these circumstances meeting in any other quarter of the realm would hardly have produced much better effects".*

St Michael's Mount, 1540

24th July 1595

DAYBREAK found Carlos de Amézola's galleys about 15 miles offshore and, from there, they made their way into Mount's Bay to anchor again off the Western Green between the smouldering ruins of Penzance and Newlyn.

It was the Eve of St Dominic's Day, and the principal chaplain of the galleys, Friar Domingo Martinez, himself of the Dominican Order, asked leave of the commander to celebrate Mass ashore. Amézola was pleased to grant permission. With help, the Friar set up a hut with an altar and cross.

Fearful curiosity had made many local people venture out onto the hills overlooking the Western Green, giving the commander concern that some might be armed, and possibly endanger those taking part in the service. His solution to this was quite simple, organising several musketeers and arquebusiers to let off a salvo of shots in celebration of the Mass being held on the soil of Elizabeth Tudor's Protestant realm. This also created a very effective deterrent to any show of bravado from the locals. After his release by the Spaniards, Barnaby Loe asserted that his captors had vowed to build a priory on the site of the Mass after Spain had won the war.

Whether this event explains the place-name Mennaye, applied to the area of the Pirates rugby football ground on what was once the Western Green, can only be conjectured. It derives from Cornish: *meneghi*, "church-land", but no other church or chapel of any antiquity is recorded in the immediate vicinity.

Richard Carew wrote a curious account of this day, which would seem to be pure fiction. He claimed that the Spaniards threatened to land but did not do so because some local people had turned up to fire bullets and arrows into the galleys which were then forced to move further offshore. Amézola made no mention of his galleys coming under any fire, and his account of the day was confirmed afterwards by Barnaby Loe. Carew could only have been given this account by Sir Francis Godolphin who was then encamped four or five miles away on the west side of Marazion, from where he could not have seen any of the activities on the Western Green.

Carlos de Amézola had a second concern, regarding the single gun in the shore battery at Penzance, and which had remained intact. Anxious that it should not be used against his flotilla, he ordered Sergeant-Major Juan de Arnica to take a launch with a dozen musketeers and arquebusiers to capture the gun, and remove it. Although some men appeared to make a show of defending the gun, the threat of the landing party's firepower was enough to dissuade them, and the gun was duly manhandled aboard the launch and brought out to the flagship.

After Mass had been completed, and all personnel had returned to the galleys, the flotilla put back to sea. A vessel had been spotted in the direction of the Lizard, and the captain thought it would amuse his men to give chase to her. Within two hours, the vessel found itself within range of the galleys' guns and hove-to. It was found that this vessel was Irish, laden with wine and salt, and the captain allowed her to go on her way unharmed, after purchasing a butt of wine, before the galleys again returned to their mooring position off the Western Green.

Western Green between Newlyn and Penzance, 1540

25th July 1595

IT would seem that the men who had unsuccessfully attempted to prevent the shore battery gun from being taken by Juan de Urbea's men had been taken prisoner and brought aboard the flagship. Captain de Amézola wrote that he interrogated some local men who had been taken prisoner on land. From them, he learned that Sir Francis Godolphin was on his way with 8,000 men to prevent any more landings and damage from the Spanish galleys.

Whether this was true or not, it was serious food for thought and Captain de Amézola now had several things on his mind. This was now his third day in Mount's Bay, and the longer he stayed, the greater the risk of a Royal Navy fleet arriving from Plymouth. His men had found no trace, in any of the warehouses and stores in Mousehole, Newlyn or Penzance, of the booty that had been captured from Pernambuco by Admiral Lancaster. Amézola concluded that it had been taken to London and was, therefore, out of reach.

Moreover, his vice-flagship or *patrona*, the galley *Salvador*, had sprung a sizeable leak. How this had happened is not explained: the galleys had not come under any fire and it may be that she had struck a submerged rock off the Western Green, perhaps the Wherry Rocks, or The Gear which lay off the shore battery. She was taking in water and there were no safe facilities for repairing her in the bay. The only choice open to him would be to shepherd her back across the mouth of the Channel to Pouldavid, although this would mean abandoning any attempt to assess the Isles of Scilly, as had been intended.

Barnaby Loe, Robert Kettell and Carew all made mention of a shortage of potable water aboard the galleys, but this is difficult to believe as the Spaniards had secured unhindered access to both the Newlyn River and the Lariggan stream.

Having made his decision, Carlos de Amézola decided to release all of his prisoners, and put them safely ashore. He wrote that Captain Richard Burley had remarked that the Catholics among them would have been pleased at what the galleys had achieved, and would quickly release the news to other Catholics in the country who would also be very glad to hear it.

Having released the prisoners unharmed, it was the prudent time to leave. Even if some objectives had not been achieved, the raid had been an unqualified success and had dealt a huge blow to Elizabeth Tudor and her military commanders. There was still no sign of the Royal Navy (although Carew asserted that some ships were closing on the Lizard) and so the galleys put to sea aided by a north-north-westerly wind. It was a timely departure as, on Marazion Green, Sir Francis Godolphin had now received reinforcements from Plymouth led by Sir Nicholas Clifford, Sir Hugh Power and other captains.

It is not known if the Royal Navy was on its way to Mount's Bay or had even left Plymouth, but the Spanish galleys caught no sight of their ships.

As they left Mount's Bay, the galleys sighted two ships and gave chase, catching them at 5pm. Both turned out to be Scottish vessels and, again Captain de Amézola allowed them to go on their way unharmed, but not before gaining some valuable information.

The Scotsmen had seen a Dutch fleet off the Pointe du Raz, which potentially meant some rich pickings. The galleys sailed on throughout the night, in fair weather.

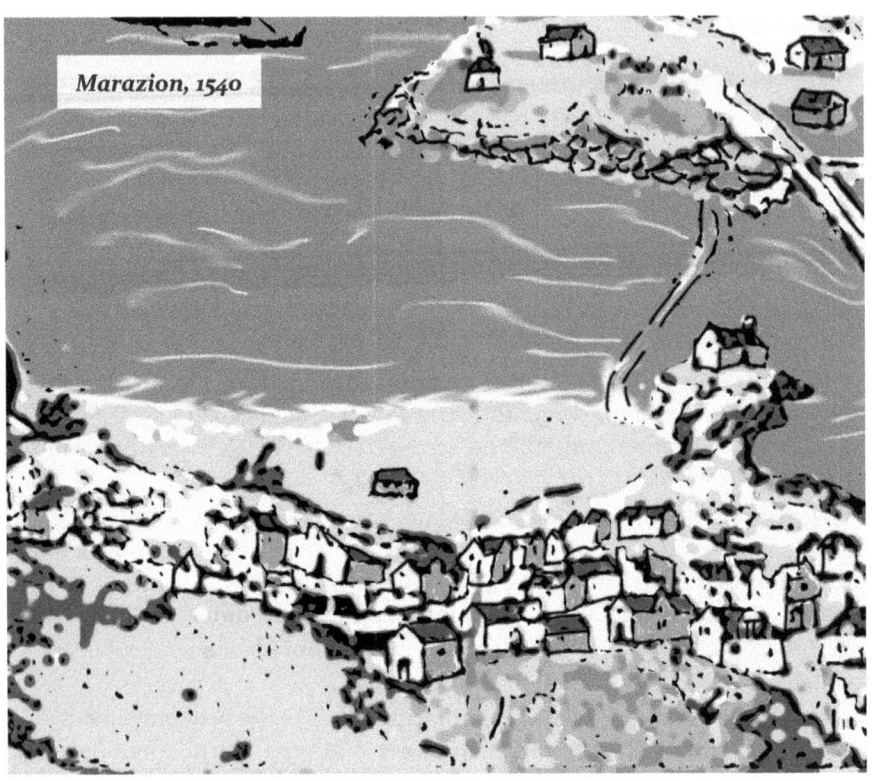

Marazion, 1540

26th July 1595

THE information offered by the Scotsmen proved to be accurate, and it was at dawn that galleys sighted the Dutch fleet. In all, this convoy consisted of 46 ships, sailing in close formation, seven of them being well-armed escorts to the merchantmen. It was a tough proposition to attack such a fleet with four galleys, one of them leaking badly, but Captain Carlos de Amézola did not hesitate.

The galleys moved in with the wind at their backs, and opened fire. The fleet escort vessels responded in kind. As four of these escorts had dropped behind the rest, Amézola singled one out, and took the *Nuestra Señora de Begoña* in, firing all cannons, and with a boarding party at the ready. 16 Spanish soldiers leapt aboard the Dutch vessel, with Juan Gómez, a subaltern of Captain Don Léon de Ezpeleta, taking a pike wound to the thigh. On approach, three puffs of smoke had been seen aboard the Dutch ship and the landing party found this to have been a signal to scuttle the ship by exploding a quantity of gunpowder which had been placed on deck. Seeing this, the landing party quickly returned to the galley, after setting light to the powder themselves and blowing up the deck.

The *Nuestra Señora de Begoña*'s cannons then sent the ship to the bottom with all hands bar one, who was seen floundering in the water and was picked up by the galley's launch. The sunken ship had been estimated at 250 tons, with over 50 men aboard, all servicemen, and had been armed by ten artillery pieces; the other six escort vessels being of similar size and armament.

Meanwhile the *Peregrina* had put a boarding party aboard a second vessel, while men from the *Bazana* boarded a third, supported by the *Salvador*, which had been lagging behind due to the amount of water she was shipping. Under her captain Juan de Mercado, the *Peregrina*'s attack had been ferocious, ripping her Dutch opponent open and killing half of her complement. Seeing that her opponent was finished, the gunners ceased fire to allow her to sink, the subaltern Juan de Urbea sending a skiff to pick up the boarding party, and not a moment too soon.

By now, the galleys had suffered damage. The flagship had a shattered foremast and a cannonball had severed the *Peregrina*'s mainmast, while she had also taken three hits near her bow, causing her to ship water. A freshening wind was allowing three of the Dutch escorts to move in against the *Peregrina*, which withdrew alongside the *Bazana*.

Assessing the situation, Amézola ordered his galleys to pull back from the fleet and regroup. He found that his own flotilla had lost 20 men in the engagement, with several more wounded. The Dutch fleet had now gathered around the ship that was sinking, the other having already sunk.

At that point, the commander decided it prudent to break off the attack and resume course for Pouldavid, which all four galleys reached safely at dusk to anchor in its safe harbour, despite two of them suffering from bad leaks.

A subsequent letter by Thomas Treffry contains a none-too-accurate report of this engagement and no one can be certain where he could have found the information. This asserts that the Dutch fleet had 70 ships, not 46, with 14 detached from the rest, and not the 4 specified by Amézola. Treffry also claimed that one of the galleys was so badly damaged that the Spaniards had been forced to abandon her, whereas it is clear that, despite two having serious leaks, all four safely reached Pouldavid. He was also to claim that 140 Spaniards had been killed in the exchange, but the fact was that Amézola lost 20 men, his only casualties of the entire venture.

30th July 1595

JUAN del Aguila's report states that that the galleys underwent repairs at Penmarc'h, although Pouldavid is a far more likely location for this to have taken place as Penmarc'h offers little in the way of shelter or resources for ship repair. The *Salvador* badly needed her leaking hull to be patched up; the *Nuestra Señora de Begoña* required a new foremast; and the *Peregrina* was in need of a new mainmast and repairs to the shot damage to her bow. The *Bazana* seems to have been unscathed. If she was the same *Bazana* that had survived the Armada disaster seven years earlier, then she was indeed a lucky ship.

They set out again on the 30th July, arriving at Blavet at dusk without further incident. *"Here,"* Captain Carlos de Amézola wrote his report to King Philip II, *"the galleys remain, ready to serve Your Majesty in whatever way is deemed most convenient".*

The Effects of the Raid

THE Spanish raid on Mount's Bay had achieved something the Armada could not. For two and half days, Spanish forces had actually controlled a corner of the realm administered by Elizabeth Tudor, the first invasion of Britain from foreign shores for several centuries.

As mentioned, commentators who were not present spoke harshly of cowardice among the local people, but these had not been soldiers. They were poorly equipped farmers, fisherfolk, miners and townspeople faced by up to 400 heavily armed, highly trained and disciplined soldiers backed by heavy artillery from four ships.

Sir Francis Godolphin's account to Richard Carew could be construed as the report of a man desperate to defend his own rather shambolic part, most of which was spent well back from the action on Marazion Green. Although Sir Nicholas Clifford was to back Godolphin by reporting (with more than a touch of class snobbery): *"As for the town of Penzance, had the people stood with Sir Francis Godolphin, who engaged himself very worthily, it (would) have (been) saved, but the common sort utterly forsook him, saving four or five gentlemen"*, Sir Thomas Baskerville's view was rather more damning of Godolphin: *"If any captain of judgement had been there to conduct the people, with only 200 men, and had accosted the enemy in flank, the country would have saved from spoil and fire, and without any loss; had they attempted it whilst the enemy followed the spoil in the sacking of the towns, then disorder would have undoubtedly overthrown them."*

Godolphin was also terrified of Spanish intentions towards the Isles of Scilly, which also fell under his command: *"I gather by the desire these Spaniards have to Scilly that, if they can possess it, they will keep their galleys there under the fort: from their present attempt I observe that the principal want is two good pieces* (of ordnance) *to beat them from The Road, and a better store of powder, bullets and match, with some skilful and valiant leaders, which will be needful in all places where the Spaniards may do hurt in their landing".*

The local people were also mindful of the prophecy that had allegedly been uttered by Merlin a thousand years earlier:

Y a wra tira war'n Men Merlyn,
A wra lesky Pawl, Pensans ha Lulyn.

They shall land on the stone of Merlin,
Who shall burn Paul, Penzance and Newlyn.

Admittedly, the earliest known reference to this prophecy is in Carew's own book, *A Survey of Cornwall* (1602), but he himself claimed that it had been known among the Cornish people for a very long time. In other words, the people knew they were facing the pre-ordained, and that there was little or nothing they could do to prevent it.

The coastal rock now named Merlin Rock on modern maps and charts is not the original, which lay under the later extension of Mousehole's south quay, the very spot upon which the Spanish forces landed on the morning of the 23rd July 1595.

The death toll appears to have been very low. The Spanish forces lost no men at all during the raid, their only casualties occurring during the fight with the Dutch convoy on the way home.

Among the Cornish, only three deaths are known for sure, with a possible fourth. John Tremearne, vicar of Paul, was to record in his new register (the old one having been lost in the burning of the church) the burials of: Jenkin Keigwin of *"Moussel, being killed by the Spaniards"*; and John Pearce Peiton, both on the 24th July 1595; and Jacobus (James) of Newlyn, *"was killed by enemies and buried"*, and *"similarly Teck Cornall was buried"*, both being interred two days later. Keeping the body count as low as humanly possible seems to been high on the Spanish agenda, almost certainly an intention to gain support from Cornish Catholics.

Across the bay, the burgesses of wealthy and newly chartered Marazion saw the burning wreck of Penzance, and could be forgiven for thinking that it could never again rise from the ashes to the point where it could compete with its own commercial success. The very opposite was to hold true. Like the mythical phoenix, and to the lasting detriment of Marazion, Penzance was not only rebuilt, but grew and gained Borough status for itself within 19 years of its destruction.

It could be argued that the resolve and ambition of the Penzance townsfolk to rebuild the town and forge a new and ambitious future for it, was triggered by the actions of Captain Carlos de Amézola and his four galleys.

References

- Carew, Richard, **The Survey of Cornwall**, 1602
- Dickinson, Robert, **The Spanish Raid on Mount's Bay in 1595**, JRIC 1988
- Graham, Graham, **The Spanish Armadas**, 1972
- Halliday, F. E., **A History of Cornwall**, 1959
- **Library of Congress, Washington DC, USA**
- Pool, P. A. S., **History of Penzance**, 1974
- Rowse, A. L., **Tudor Cornwall**, 1941
- **State Papers of the Reign of Elizabeth I**
- **State Papers of the Reign of Philip II**
- **The National Archives**

Lightning Source UK Ltd.
Milton Keynes UK
UKHW020911300819
348617UK00002B/5/P